MW01070869

This book belongs to

Please read it to me.
Thank you!

Ellie

Bitsy

Pickles
and the Family Reunion

Written by Joan K. Moore

Illustrated by Cheyanne Montano

© 2016 Copyright

Published by Idea Storm Press
Lake Zurich, Illinois
Copyright © 2016 by Joan K. Moore.
Library of Congress Control Number: 2016938203

All rights reserved. No part of this book may be reproduced, scanned,
or distributed in any printed or electronic form without permission.
Please do not participate in or encourage piracy of copyrighted
materials in violation of the author's right.
Purchase only authorized editions.

ISBN: 978-1-945313-00-4

www.jkmhappy.com

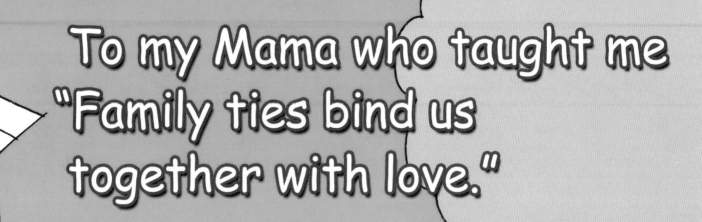

To my Mama who taught me "Family ties bind us together with love."

Characters...

Tiny
(Pickles' Mother)

Mr. Sims
(Pickles' Dad)

Bodine
(Pickles' Brother)

Wilson

Pickles
(Daughter of Tiny & Mr. Sims)

Mama Belle lives in a big farmhouse in Kettle, Kentucky. Her cats, Mr. Sims and Tiny, and their kittens, Pickles and Bodine, live in the barn on the farm.

They were all one, big, happy family.

Until one day...

Mama Belle's sister Susan and her dog Wilson arrived from Chicago, Illinois.

"Welcome to Kentucky, Wilson! I am glad you could come to the family reunion. Congratulations on winning your spelling bee and making the honor roll," Tiny said.

While Tiny talked to Wilson, Pickles listened and played with a rope. She batted a few stray strands. Pickles wanted Tiny to say how well she could read and do math.

Instead, Tiny scolded, "Pickles, now is not the time to play. Say hello to Wilson and go get ready for the family reunion feast! Wilson must be hungry after his long trip."

Reluctantly, Pickles cast aside the rope and said, "Hi Wilson."

"Mama likes Wilson more than me," Pickles whined to Bodine.

Bodine said, "Wilson is smart. Mama is recognizing him for his accomplishments."

"But she does not recognize me. I get good grades in school and I am pretty and playful," Pickles said as she fluffed her tail.

Pickles felt Mama did not love her.

"I will go live with a family

who wants a kitten like me."

That night Pickles waited until she heard the loud snore of Mr. Sims before she sneaked out of bed, tiptoed across the barn, and climbed out a window.

It was dark outside.

Pickles did not know where she was going, but

knew she did not belong on the farm.

Pickles had not gone far when it started to rain very hard. She disliked getting wet. As she heard a clap of thunder, a strong wind blew sticks and leaves everywhere.

Thinking of her warm bed, Pickles cried, "I want to go home!"

Pickles started running as fast as she could.

Where was the barn?

She could not see anything but darkness.

She was soaking wet and lost!

When Mr. Sims and Tiny heard the thunder, they checked on everyone.

Bodine was hiding under the hay. Wilson was sleeping.

Where was Pickles?

"Pickles, where are you?" called Mr. Sims and Tiny.

No answer. They did not see her anywhere.

"Don't worry, Tiny," Mr. Sims said. "I will find her. She can't be far in this storm."

Wilson jumped up and said, "I will help!"

Mr. Sims tucked his ears against his head
and ran out of the barn.

Wilson sniffed the ground to find Pickles' scent. He
followed Mr. Sims and yelled, "Pickles,"
over and over again.

Pickles heard Wilson calling. A strike of lightning gave her enough light to see the barn. She ran toward it, but fell in a deep hole. The hole was filled with thick, slimy mud and she got stuck.

"Help!" Pickles cried. "Help me, please!"

Pickles had never been so scared.

Would anyone save her?

Wilson heard Pickles cry and discovered she was stuck. He quickly ran to the barn and grabbed the rope Pickles had abandoned. As Wilson pulled her out of the hole, Pickles was shivering.

Safe and back in the barn, Pickles said,

"Thank you very much Wilson for rescuing me."

Wilson said, "You are welcome."

spoke lovingly to Pickles. "Please do not run away again. You belong here with us. Remember the rope Wilson used to rescue you?"

"Yes Mama," Pickles said.

"The rope has strands that bind together to make it strong. Pickles, we are family and we are strong together. Family ties bind us together with love. There are two ways to know you are loved. I show you and I tell you. I love you my sweet little kitten."

Pickles could not believe her ears.

Mama really did love her!

Pickles was home where she belonged and the family had a very happy reunion.

Feeling tired, Pickles settled down for
a long, cozy nap.

When she woke up, Pickles looked around the
barn. She loved each of the animals, even Wilson.
Pickles smiled and said, "As Mama says, family ties
bind us together with love."

Written by
Joan K. Moore

Joan grew up in Kettle, Kentucky, and now lives in Schaumburg, Illinois. She is the aunt of two terrific nephews, four fabulous nieces, one great-niece and one great-nephew.

Joan's mother taught her simple truths and valuable life lessons, which inspired her to begin writing children's books. Pickles was one of the numerous cats owned by her mother.

Illustrated by
Cheyanne Montano

Cheyanne is 14 years old and an 8th grader at Liberty Jr. High School. She lives in New Lenox, Illinois with her parents and silly cat Maya.

She enjoys reading, drawing, hiking, and competing with her horse Ellie. Cheyanne loved illustrating Pickles and the Family Reunion.

Questions

1. Name the characters in the book Pickles and the Family Reunion.

2. What was the setting for the story?

3. What challenge was Pickles facing?

4. What lesson did Pickles learn from her Mama?

5. Who rescued Pickles?

ANSWERS: 1. Tiny, Mr. Sims, Pickles, Bodine, and Wilson; 2. Mama Belle's farm in Kettle, Kentucky; 3. She felt Mama did not love her; 4. Family ties bind us together with love; 5. Wilson

Also available...

available at amazon.com

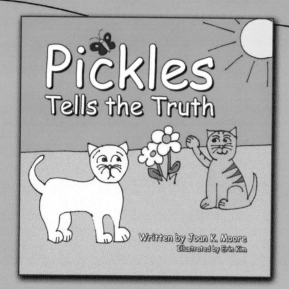

Pickles
Tells the Truth

Written by Joan K. Moore
Illustrated by Erin Kim

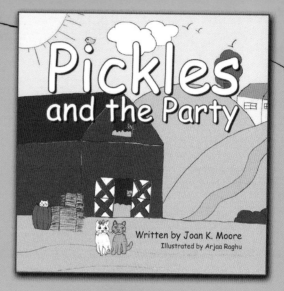

Pickles
and the Party

Written by Joan K. Moore
Illustrated by Arjaa Raghu

P-i-c-k-l-e-s Spells Pickles

Written by
Joan K. Moore

Illustrated by
Isaiah Ortiz

55618754R00030

Made in the USA
Charleston, SC
01 May 2016

Mama says...

Family Ties Bind Us Together With Love.

www.jkmhappy.com

ISBN 978-1-945313-00-4

9 781945 313004